Winter Fun

LET'S GO SLEDDING!

By Jasper Bix

Gareth Stevens
PUBLISHING

Please visit our website, www.garethstevens.com. For a free color catalog of all our high-quality books, call toll free 1-800-542-2595 or fax 1-877-542-2596.

Library of Congress Cataloging-in-Publication Data

Bix, Jasper.
Let's go sledding! / Jasper Bix.
pages cm. — (Winter Fun)
Includes index.
ISBN 978-1-4824-3759-1 (pbk.)
ISBN 978-1-4824-3760-7 (6 pack)
ISBN 978-1-4824-3761-4 (library binding)
1. Sledding—Juvenile literature. I. Title. II. Title: Let us go sledding.
GV856.B58 2016
796.9'5—dc23
2015023144

First Edition

Published in 2016 by
Gareth Stevens Publishing
111 East 14th Street, Suite 349
New York, NY 10003

Editor: Ryan Nagelhout
Designer: Sarah Liddell

Photo credits: Cover, pp. 1, 9, 13, 21 Air Images/Shutterstock.com; pp. 5, 7 Artens/Shutterstock.com; p. 11 djgis/Shutterstock.com; pp. 15, 24 (sled) Sandra van der Steen/Shutterstock.com; pp. 17, 24 (saucer) BlueSkyImage/Shutterstock.com; pp. 19, 24 (snow tube) tammykayphoto/Shutterstock.com; p. 23 Frederick Bass/Getty Images.

Printed in the United States of America

CPSIA compliance information: Batch #CW16GS: For further information contact Gareth Stevens, New York, New York at 1-800-542-2595.

Contents

It snowed last night!

We want
to go sledding.

We wear warm clothes.

We need a tall hill
to sled down!

We walk up the hill.

Our sled is
made of wood.

Other sleds are
round and flat.
They are called saucers.

Some people use things filled with air! This is called snow tubing.

I get on the sled.
It's time to go downhill!

I go down very fast.
I want to do it again!

Words to Know

saucer

sled

snow tube

Index